TODAY GOD SAYS I AM

Publishing & Printing

Mission: To Proclaim Transformation and Truth
Publisher: Transformed Publishing, Cocoa, FL
Website: www.transformedpublishing.com
Email: transformedpublishing@gmail.com

Copyright © 2025 by Briley Jo Cruz

All rights reserved solely by the author. No part of this book may be reproduced, stored in a retrieval system, or transmitted in any form or by any means without expressed written permission of the author.

Cover image is an original photograph provided by author. Additional interior images were retrieved from Storyblocks.com via publisher's subscription allowance.

This work is based on the author's personal Biblical study, prayer, and inspiration of the Holy Spirit. The intention of the author is to share Scriptures and elaborate on Biblical principles that have impacted her life, in hope to inspire others. Any resemblance to someone else's life experiences, teaching, actual events or locales or persons, living or dead, is entirely coincidental.

Scriptures marked NLT are taken from: Holy Bible, New Living Translation, copyright © 1996, 2004, 2015 by Tyndale House Foundation. Used by permission of Tyndale House Publishers, Inc., Carol Stream, Illinois 60188. All rights reserved.

Scriptures marked ESV are taken from: The Holy Bible, English Standard Version. ESV® Text Edition: 2016. Copyright © 2001 by Crossway Bibles, a publishing ministry of Good News Publishers.

Scriptures marked NIV are taken from: Holy Bible, New International Version®, NIV® Copyright ©1973, 1978, 1984, 2011 by Biblica, Inc.® Used by permission. All rights reserved worldwide.

Scriptures marked NLV are taken from the New Life Version: Copyright © 1969, 2003 by Barbour Publishing, Inc.

Scriptures marked CEV are taken from the Contemporary English Version: Copyright © 1995 by American Bible Society. For more information about CEV, visit www.bibles.com and www.cev.bible.

Scriptures marked NKJV are taken from the New King James Version®. Copyright © 1982 by Thomas Nelson. Used by permission. All rights reserved.

Scriptures marked ESV are taken from: Easy-to-Read Version (ERV) Copyright © 2006 by Bible League International.

Scriptures marked GNT are taken from: Good News Translation® (Today's English Version, Second Edition) © 1992 American Bible Society. All rights reserved. For more information about GNT, visit www.bibles.com and www.gnt.bible.

Scriptures marked NASB1995 are taken from: New American Standard Bible®, Copyright © 1960, 1971, 1977, 1995 by The Lockman Foundation. All rights reserved.

ISBN: 978-1-953241-69-6 (hardcover)
ISBN: 978-1-953241-71-9 (ebook)

BRILEY JO CRUZ

TODAY GOD SAYS I AM

31 DAY DEVOTIONAL
WORKBOOK

31 IDENTITY AFFIRMATIONS GIVEN & MANDATED BY GOD

31 Identity Affirmations
Given & Mandated by God

Definitions:

GIVEN: 1. specified or stated.[1]

- identified
- set
- agreed
- decided
- designated
- named
- prearranged
- appointed

2. taking into account.[1]

- bearing in mind
- in view of
- giving consideration to
- in light of

3. a known or established fact or situation.[1]

- reality
- established fact
- certainty

MANDATED: 1. give (someone) authority to act in a certain way.[2]
2. assign (territory) . . .[2]

- assigned
- charged
- proclaimed
- ordered
- authorized
- decreed
- summoned [3]

[1, 2] Retrieved 3/16/25. https://languages.oup.com/google-dictionary-en/ Copyright © 2025 Oxford University Press. All rights reserved.
[3] Retrieved 3/16/25. https://www.thesaurus.com/ © 2025 Dictionary.com, LLC

Look at the birds.
They don't plant or harvest
or store food in barns,
for your heavenly Father feeds them.
And aren't you far more
valuable to him than they are?
-Matthew 6:26 NLT

DEDICATIONS

For my Mom,
my Dad,
and my Sister, my Best Friend—
This one's for you.
Let's keep walking together in the light
of who God says we've always been.

Table of Contents

Letter from Author	1
Provided For	2
Beloved	4
Chosen	6
Illuminated	8
Wanted	10
Confident	12
Holy	14
Week 1 Reflection	16
Invited	18
Seen	20
Guided	22
Satisfied	24
Released	26
Known	28
Befriended	30
Week 2 Reflection	32
Strengthened	34
Safe	36
Calmed	38
Forgiven	40
Clean	42
Resurrected	44
Heard	46
Week 3 Reflection	48
Hope-Full	50
Found	52
Healed	54
Hemmed In	56
Prayed For	58
Anchored	60
Fruitful	62
Week 4 Reflection	64
Equipped	66
Thought Of	68
Commissioned	70
Week 5 Final Reflection	72
Invitation	75
Prayer of Salvation	76
Acknowledgements	77
About the Author	78
Ministry Contacts	79

LETTER FROM AUTHOR

Dear reader,

WELCOME to:

TODAY GOD SAYS I AM

Know, I have already prayed for you as you've picked up this devotional, to embark on a journey of discovering, or rediscovering who God says you are; remembering what He believes about you. Rooted in His Word, each day includes a theme Bible verse, a devotional, a fill in the blank to write your name, and a journal prompt, paired with the Biblical identity affirmation for each day. Then finally, at the end of each week, there is space for a weekly reflection. Journal prompts are designed to guide the way as you pause and process what you've read that week, working through what God shows you.

The Lord once told me, "You can have as much of Me as you make room for." The more honesty, heart, and effort we put into strengthening our journey with the Lord, the deeper the Lord will do His work in us.

SO excited to be on this journey with you!

- I pray this devotional challenges you, builds up your faith, and puts on display the VAST love of God towards YOU.
- I pray it pulls back any veil causing you to believe lies about yourself and how God sees you.
- I pray it strengthens your heart and fills you with the JOY of JESUS as you begin to see more clearly, and allow Him to heal, restore, and redeem what once may have been taken.

Our God loves to, and LONGS to,
make ALL THINGS NEW.

May you feel God's presence in a fresh new way,

Briley Jo Cruz

Day #1
Today, God Says I am **Provided For**.

> He provides food for those who fear him;
> he remembers his covenant forever.
> -Psalm 111:5 ESV

My God promises to provide. He promises to provide food for m because I fear Him—not a fearful fear of Him, but instead a reverence—a look to Him—an honor Him kind of love and awe.

It is promised here in this verse that my God remembers His Covenant forever. This covenant was crafted and forged generations ago, and yet because I have accepted Him, I am now **grafted** in. When God remembers His Covenant, He remembers ME.

No matter what my need looks like today, tomorrow, or the next day, I can REST comforted and assured, taking a deep breath in and letting it all go out with it, because You say I will be provided for.

Today, God Says _____ is Provided For.

> **Provided For** Journal Prompt:
> Write down ways you need God's provision in your life.
> Thank Him in advance for working on your behalf.

_____
_____
_____
_____
_____
_____
_____

Day #2
Today, God Says I am BELOVED.

> Beloved, let us love one another, for love is from God, and whoever loves has been born of God and knows God. Anyone who does not love does not know God, because God is love.
> -1 John 4:7-8 ESV

In the New Testament times, and Hebrew culture, "Beloved" was known as a title of endearment, and closeness. As today's devotional was being written, I kept hearing "beloved", "beloved", "beloved". **"Be-Loved"**.

So today, dear reader: **Be-Loved, Beloved**.

Remember: God wants me to live today, tomorrow, and the next day, "Being-Loved". Because that's how HE sees me every minute of each day. Lord, help me live out my life from a place of knowing I'm deeply and closely loved.

Today, God Says _____ is Be-Loved.

Be-Loved Journal Prompt:
Ask yourself: In what ways can I see God express His love for me? Write down your answers.

_____
_____
_____
_____
_____
_____
_____

Day #3
Today, GOD says I am <u>chosen</u>.

> But you are a chosen people, a royal priesthood,
> a holy nation, God's special possession, that you
> may declare the praises of him who called you out
> of darkness into his wonderful light.
> -1 Peter 2:9 NIV

As I continue on this devotional journey, layers of what it means to be chosen by God will continuously be revealed to me.

But for today, Ephesians 1:4 NLT says, "Even before he made the world, God loved us and chose us in Christ to be holy and without fault in his eyes." The NLV translation writes it this way: "Even before the world was made, God chose us for Himself because of His love. He planned that we should be holy and without blame as He sees us."

As He Sees Us

My God has **chosen** me *for Himself because of His love.*
My God **chooses** me.
read that again

It's one thing to be selected one time, but as time goes by . . . mistakes made . . . things become less *shiny* than they once were. We may think we have less to offer than we once did; nevertheless, to be chosen STILL, over and over, and over again—that is real love.
My God continues to choose me.
He chooses to stand by me, to love me when I can't love myself, to stay with me when I want to run away, and still stay, the times when I do.

He called me out of darkness, into His wonderful light, and He <u>still</u> calls me out of darkness; into His wonderful light.

My God chooses me.

Today, GOD says _____ is chosen.

CHOSEN JOURNAL PROMPT:
Read Deuteronomy 31:8 in the English Standard Version. Write down how this verse encourages you with the truth that God chose you and *chooses* you still.

Day #4
Today, God Says I am ILLUMINATED.

Even in darkness light dawns for the upright,
for those who are gracious and compassionate and righteous.
-Psalm 112:4 NIV

The definition of 'illuminate' is:
1. make (something) visible or bright by shining light on it; light up
2. help to clarify or explain.

Retrieved 3/21/25. https://languages.oup.com/google-dictionary-en/
Copyright © 2025 Oxford University Press. All rights reserved.

(What an ENCOURAGEMENT!)

Even in darkness, it is promised that God will cause **LIGHT** to dawn for the upright—for His people—for His kids—FOR ME.

No matter which area of my life needs light to come into it. No matter which situation or information needs to be made visible, clarified, or explained further, God promises to **illuminate**.

Today, God Says _____ is Illuminated.

ILLUMINATED JOURNAL PROMPT:
'Illuminated' is 'to be lit with bright lights'—when you think of God being our illumination, how do you feel about that? Write down your thoughts.

Day #5
Today, God says I am <u>wanted</u>.

Even before he made the world, God loved us and chose
us in Christ to be holy and without fault in his eyes.
God decided in advance to adopt us into his own family
by bringing us to himself through Jesus Christ.
This is what he wanted to do, and it gave him great pleasure.
-Ephesians 1:4-5 NLT

Today's verse shows me the TRUTH that I am **wanted** by God.

No, this isn't the "I Want You" military sign
you may visualize from Uncle Sam.
No, it is WAY MORE and way more beautiful, and **lasting**.

When the world doesn't want me, doesn't receive me like I feel they should, and fades me into the background, I can remember, TRUST, and **believe,** my God wanted me before the beginning of time. He saw it pleasing there should be one of me orchestrated into His BIG BEAUTIFUL heart & plan.

I can THANK GOD that I am WANTED today.
Desired. Valued deeply.

God's heart is permanently set on me.

Today, God says _____ is wanted.

Wanted Journal Prompt:
Read today's key verses again.
God wanted to bring you into His family—to adopt YOU.
Can you think of a time in your life when you felt genuinely welcomed, warmly greeted, and sincerely gathered in by someone? Write about that experience, thanking God for their kindness towards you, bringing you a teeny tiny snapshot of His **vast desire** for you.

Day #6

TODAY, GOD SAYS I AM CONFIDENT.

*They are confident and fearless
and can face their foes triumphantly.*
-Psalm 112:8 NLT

The "they" in Psalm 112:8 are the "godly"—"those who fear the LORD and delight in obeying his commands" (*see* verses 1 & 4).

That's ME.

My God says I am **confident** and **fearless** and **can face my foes triumphantly**.

I can ONLY find this confidence and courage by understanding this VICTORY comes from God, and not my own doing.
This gives me RELIEF, JOY, and COMFORT knowing victory does not depend on me, what I can provide for myself, even my very best efforts.
No. This confidence, courage, and victory is given from my God who LOVES ME.

TODAY, GOD SAYS _____ IS CONFIDENT.

CONFIDENT JOURNAL PROMPT:
Read Matthew 7:24-27 in the New Living Translation.
All kinds of things in this world can shake us of our confidence, making us doubt, freeze, or fear,
but with Jesus in our hearts and lives,
our lives are built on a FIRM FOUNDATION.
How do these verses encourage you in this season of life?
Write down your thoughts.

_____
_____
_____
_____

Day #7

Today, God says I am HOLY.

For you are a people holy to the Lord your God.
The Lord your God has chosen you out of all the peoples on the face of the earth to be his people, his treasured possession.
-Deuteronomy 7:6 NIV

"Holy" is defined as dedicated or consecrated to God or a religious purpose; sacred.
<sub>Retrieved 3/21/25. https://languages.oup.com/google-dictionary-en/
Copyright © 2025 Oxford University Press. All rights reserved.</sub>

Holy, meaning **set apart**, takes the *impossible, but heavy pressure* OFF of me, to be holy, the perfect holy that only God can ascribe. When God calls me holy, it is because when He looks at me, He sees His perfect, Holy Son.

He sees JESUS, and I am thankful.
I am set apart, **holy** to the Lord my God. I have been grafted in, and *woven in. Gathered in*, to His people, His treasured possession.

Today, God says _____ is HOLY.

HOLY Journal Prompt:
Ask God if there is a new perspective on being "holy" as "being set apart" that you need to see. Is there something new about this topic He wants to teach you?
Is there a new mindset He wants to give you, a *re-write*?
He might be wanting to re-align your thinking here.
There is safe space below, let Him.

_____
_____
_____
_____
_____

WEEK 1 REFLECTION

> ### AFFIRMATIONS THIS WEEK:
> PROVIDED FOR, BELOVED, CHOSEN, ILLUMINATED, WANTED, CONFIDENT, HOLY

1. Which affirmation spoke the most to you this week? Why?

_____
_____
_____
_____
_____
_____
_____

2. Which affirmation this week could you grow in?

_____
_____
_____
_____
_____
_____
_____

Note: The following prompt is not a *one and done*—my prayer is that this lays the groundwork for you to continue to return here to this practice: Listing the lies we're listening to and then listing the truths of what God says about you in His Word contradicting those lies. God continues to pull back layers of things we've adopted along the way that were never meant for us to carry; labels that didn't come from Him and were never meant for us to wear as our own.

With this said, complete this prompt with a willing heart and open hands; *being still* to hear God's voice speaking to *you*.

3. Are there any lies you've been believing that may have popped up this week while reading?
- List them.
- Talk to God about them.
- Replace them with God's truth.
- Thank God in advance for HELPING you live your life through a new lens of truth.

Day #8
Today, God says I am <u>Invited</u>.

"Come, follow me," Jesus said, "and I will send you out to fish for people." At once they left their nets and followed him.
-Matthew 4:19-20 NIV

THE BEST INVITATION
TO THE BEST PARTY YOU'LL EVER RECEIVE

I am INVITED.

From before the foundations of the earth, my God was dreaming of the day I would accept His invitation. My *Salvation Invitation*– that was JUST the beginning! God, my Heavenly Father, CONTINUES to invite me to partner & participate in His good plan, telling others of ALL He's done & of His VAST incomprehensible LOVE for mankind.

"Come, follow me" . . .
and at once they left their nets and followed him.

Lord, I hear You.
I hear, again, Your invitation to partner WITH You.
Help me leave "my nets" *at once* and follow you today.

Today, God says _____ is Invited.

Invited Journal Prompt:
What are my "nets" God might be asking me to leave today?

_____
_____
_____
_____
_____
_____

Day #9
TODAY, GOD SAYS I AM <u>SEEN</u>.

She gave this name to the Lord who spoke to her:
"You are the God who sees me," for she said,
"I have now seen the One who sees me."
-Genesis 16:13 NIV

The woman in today's passage of Scripture found herself with nothing, in a literal wilderness *wasteland*, and yet it was HERE that God revealed to her a new facet of His character.

Just as *she* said, I can *trustfully* say, "My God sees me."

I am **seen**, and *looked after*, like this woman came to realize.

. . . for she said,
"Truly here I have seen him who looks after me."
-Gen. 16:13 ESV

When the world doesn't see me, I am seen, *still*. When the world passes me by, my God is at a one-glance-away distance from me. When I feel uncared about, I can take a deep breath, *pause*, and remember—I am *forever looked after*.

TODAY, GOD SAYS _____ IS SEEN.

SEEN JOURNAL PROMPT:
Hagar found herself in a literal wasteland with her son at the end of the line, as far as she saw.
If you are in a wasteland of any kind in your life right now, offer God a prayer—write it out—now being reminded that HE is a God who sees and a God who comes to us even in our most deserted places.

_____
_____
_____

Day #10

TODAY, GOD SAYS I AM <u>GUIDED</u>.

I praise you, Lord, for being my guide.
Even in the darkest night, your teachings fill my mind.
-Psalm 16:7 CEV

In a world that feels like it's getting darker and darker, colder, and colder, there are multiple Scriptures to turn to, to see God as my guide, but one story in particular comes to mind.

The LORD spread a cloud above them as a covering
and gave them a great fire to light the darkness.
-Psalm 105:39 NLT

The LORD guided the people of Israel through the wilderness by revealing His covering and His light to them.
With the very same heart, the LORD promises to do this for me.

Even in the darkest night, Your teachings fill my mind.

Help me remember, LORD.

TODAY, GOD SAYS _____ IS GUIDED.

<u>GUIDED</u> JOURNAL PROMPT:
After reading Psalm 16:7-8, <u>start with one</u> teaching, one Bible verse, one Biblical truth for you to spend some time on. Write it down here, so that in your darkest night, God might bring this verse out of you, as a light guiding your way.

_____
_____
_____
_____
_____
_____

Day #11

TODAY, GOD SAYS I AM <u>SATISFIED</u>.

The Lord will guide you always;
he will satisfy your needs in a sun-scorched land
and will strengthen your frame.
You will be like a well-watered garden,
like a spring whose waters never fail.
-Isaiah 58:11 NIV

Of the many things I can take away from this verse,
one thing I can pick up on is this **comparison:**
the description of hardship versus the description
of God satisfying me, *within* the hardship.

My location doesn't change . . .
God is promising to **satisfy** me WITHIN the location.

In a sun scorched land, my God promises to satisfy my needs.
In a trying, weary, and tearful place, season, or year(s);
my God promises to *strengthen my frame.*
He says to me: *I will be like a well-watered garden,
like a spring whose waters never fail.*

In times when this is easy to believe, and times when it isn't,
my God's Word never fails, and HE never fails me either.
HE will Satisfy.

TODAY, GOD SAYS _____ IS SATISFIED.

<u>SATISFIED</u> JOURNAL PROMPT:
God's presence & His Word will satisfy YOU.
Is there a specific Word, promise, or Bible verse
God has spoken to you or led you to?
1. If He has, revisit that place today.
Write those words here in this space.
2. If it has been a while since He's spoken to you or if this
is your first time, ask Him to satisfy you with His Word.

Day #12
Today, God Says I am Released.

*He led them from the darkness and deepest gloom;
he snapped their chains.*
-Psalm 107:14 NLT

The entire 107th chapter of Psalms tells the reader of the FAITHFUL ways God has come through for His people, while in *exile*.

Though they found themselves wandering, living in a place that was not their home, **every time** they cried out "LORD, help!", *'He saved them from their distress'.*

(Today's verse should GET ME EXCITED!)
No matter how thick the darkness feels around me, nor the deepest gloom that sets in, my God is CAPABLE and READY TO SNAP MY CHAINS just as He did for His people, in days of old.

My God is in the business of *Snapping Chains & Releasing Prisoners.* He's in the business of *Breaking Down Prison Mentalities* . . . and He's **one,** "LORD, help!" away.

Today, God Says _____ is Released.

Released Journal Prompt:
Go somewhere quiet and ask yourself these questions:
1. Are there chains right now in my life God wants to snap for me?
2. Are there chains He has snapped that I'm still holding on to?

_____
_____
_____
_____

Day #13
TODAY, GOD SAYS I AM <u>KNOWN</u>.

O Lord, You have searched me and known *me*.
-Psalm 139:1 NKJV

He knows *how* I grew up, *what* I've come through, and *beautifully, who* I will be at the end of my story, crossing into eternity.

God's Perfect Knowledge of Man, is the title of this Psalm in the New King James Translation, and it fits the heart of this passage like a warm winter glove.

I am **KNOWN**.

God's Perfect Knowledge of Man, extends to me, leaping off the pages of Psalm 139, to wrap me up with the truth of this love. I am **perfectly known** & I am **perfectly loved**. It has ALWAYS been this way and it will ALWAYS be.

As mankind, we can't truly wrap our minds around what perfect love is, *but* as we walk in step with the Lord, day by day, we are given *glimpses* and *imaginations* of just how *beautiful* that gift *will be* when we can *know* it in *full* expression.

TODAY, GOD SAYS _____ IS KNOWN.

> ### <u>KNOWN</u> JOURNAL PROMPT:
> Spend some time in Psalm 139 today.
> Ask God to show you at least one new thing in His Word today. (He surely wants to.)

_____
_____
_____
_____
_____

Day #14
TODAY, GOD SAYS I AM <u>BEFRIENDED</u>.

> God is faithful, who has called you into
> fellowship with his Son, Jesus Christ our Lord.
> -1 Corinthians 1:9 NIV

What a profound statement.

The God of the entire universe has called me into fellowship—**friendship**—relationship with Jesus, His Son.

I am befriended by the One whom Scripture says:

> For of Him and through Him and to Him *are* all things,
> to whom *be* glory forever. Amen.
> -Romans 11:36 NKJV

My God has called me in. He has gathered me.
I am *included* and *desired*.

Some days it is easy to feel alone, or lonely in this world, but my God wants me to remember I am befriended by He who made the heavens, the Earth, the mountains, and the seas.

TODAY, GOD SAYS _____ IS BEFRIENDED.

BEFRIENDED JOURNAL PROMPT:
Read John 15:13 in the New Living Translation. Jesus became the fulfillment of that verse with YOU in mind—*if it was just for you*—He still would have done it.

1. Can you think of a time when you felt, or were, unfriended by others?
2. Reflecting on that experience, ask the Lord to heal the hurt surrounding it, knowing your God was with you in that moment then, and is with you, in this moment now.

WEEK 2 REFLECTION

> **AFFIRMATIONS THIS WEEK:**
> INVITED, SEEN, GUIDED, SATISFIED,
> RELEASED, KNOWN, BEFRIENDED

1. Which affirmation spoke the most to you this week? Why?

   _____
   _____
   _____
   _____
   _____
   _____
   _____

2. Which affirmation this week could you grow in?

   _____
   _____
   _____
   _____
   _____
   _____
   _____
   _____

3. Are there any lies you've been believing that may have popped up this week while reading?
   - List them.
   - Talk to God about them.
   - Replace them with God's truth.
   - Thank God in advance for HELPING you live your life through a new lens of truth.

Day #15
Today, God Says I Am <u>Strengthened</u>.

I will love You, O Lord, my strength.
The Lord is my rock and my fortress and my deliverer;
My God, my strength, in whom I will trust;
My shield and the horn of my salvation, my stronghold.
-Psalm 18:1-2 NKJV

In times of weakness and weariness,
I have a strength that does not reside in human ability.
I have access to a power that does not come from human hands,
but rather from the **Spirit of the Living God**.

My God is my strength.
My God is my strength.
My God is my strength.
(Say it till you believe it, my soul.)

THANK YOU, for being my strength today, God.
I open my hands, letting go the grip of control.
You, God, are trustworthy.
My God, my strength, in whom I will trust.

Today, God Says _____ Is Strengthened.

Strengthened Journal Prompt:
Write down a prayer offering to God asking Him for help
to tap into *His* strength this week, remembering and standing
on His abilities, and not *only* on what you have to offer.
Remembering, *Who* your God is.
How has He been faithful to you in the past?
Remember His faithfulness.

_____
_____
_____

Day #16
Today, God Says I am <u>Safe</u>.

In peace I will lie down and sleep,
for you alone, Lord, make me dwell in safety.
-Psalm 4:8 NIV

Ever had a restless night? . . . Or two, or five, or 10?

When the world is weighing me down,
and my thoughts are running faster than I can chase them,
as I lay on my pillow, I have a promise to speak *to the night*.

This promise comes from a Psalm of David.
Many of the ebbs and flows of his days are widely known,
and I can *picture him*, in my mind's eye, *lying down*,
tucked away in a cave on the cliff of a mountain,
speaking this truth over himself, too.
Speaking it till he believes it.

My Lord, alone, makes me dwell in safety.
In sleeping or awake, safety *belongs* to Him.
You, God are my rock,
". . . my hiding place high in the hills."
-Psalm 18:2 ERV

Today, God Says _____ is Safe.

Safe Journal Prompt:
If nighttime is a hard time for you, commit today's verse to memory, and speak it over yourself when you lay down to sleep. Write it on a sticky note or flash card. Place it somewhere you can see it. Whisper it out loud and believe in God's faithfulness to YOU.

_____
_____
_____
_____

Day #17
TODAY, GOD SAYS I AM <u>CALMED</u>.

Then He arose and rebuked the wind, and said to the sea, "Peace, be still!" And the wind ceased and there was a great calm
-Mark 4:39 NKJV

The people, in my boat, matter!

I can rest in knowing that there is no safer place for me than close to my Jesus.

I am perfectly placed for every storm when I see *whose* Spirit lives *inside* me! The same Spirit of God who resided in Jesus, now resides in me and if God's Spirit enabled Jesus to calm the storm with three words, I am positioned well, no matter the circumstance, no matter the amount of fear.

The storm *may* rage on for me, but as God's child, I *will* be calmed. I will be comforted, *within the storm*. God promises to quiet me, in my fight, flight, or freeze.

With His love He will calm all my fears.
-*see* Zephaniah 3:17 NLT

TODAY, GOD SAYS _____ IS CALMED.

CALMED JOURNAL PROMPT:
Is there a situation in your life right now where you need the calm of Jesus to overshadow the fear you feel in your heart?

Talk to God about it. He's closer than you know. Find one Bible verse to cling to, in faith, assuring you God will calm your heart & calm your mind.

_____
_____
_____
_____

Day #18

Today, God says I am **Forgiven**.

As far as the east is from the west,
so far does he remove our sins from us.
-Psalm 103:12 GNT

(This is Good News.)

A line in a movie once said,
"Forgiveness is setting a prisoner free.
And you realize the prisoner was you."

Jesus did the unthinkable, giving His life—His breath—on the cross,
to remove our sins from us, so we can have access to the Father,
redeemed of our wrongs, and *invited* into the family of God.

I am forgiven.

And with this *gift* of forgiveness, I can forgive others, too.
Lord, though this sacred ground is hard and holy,
help me forgive someone today. Show me a name, a face.
Is it someone else, or is it me—do I need to forgive myself today?

Lord, wash me. Lead me, guide me, and show me the way *forward*.
Thank You for *equipping* me with everything I need to forgive.
In Jesus' name, Amen.

Today, God says _____ is Forgiven.

Forgiven Journal Prompt:
Set some quiet time aside to pause, think, and talk to God about forgiveness. Is there someone you need to forgive?
The time is now.
Talk to Him: "Lord, bring a name to memory."
"Lord, do I need to forgive myself?"

_____
_____
_____

Day #19
TODaY, GOD SaYS I aM CLean.

Jesus reached out his hand and touched the man.
"I am willing," he said. "Be clean!"
Immediately he was cleansed of his leprosy.
-Matthew 8:3 NIV

Matthew chapter 8 verses 1-4 present two beautiful miracles.
The first miracle is one of a *physical* nature,
a *battered body* is cleansed and made new,
but the second miracle restores at an even *deeper* level.
The second miracle? A *broken man* is liberated.
Liberation from shame, isolation, grief over loss,
embarrassment, inflicted loneliness.

And God offers me the same liberation from my sins.
He's already done it!
When I said *yes* to Jesus, asking Him inside,
God began to see me spotless!
He sees me through His Son—clean; hidden securely in Jesus.

I serve a miracle-working God who loves me.
Whether I'm needing a physical cleansing, a broken-spirit
liberation, or a cleansing of my heart through forgiveness,
my God is a miracle-working God who desires to make me clean.
I can trust Him with me.

TODaY, GOD SaYS _____ IS CLean.

CLean Journal Prompt:
Read Isaiah 1:18 today. I really like the wording of the
New International Version translation for this verse.
Our God has **settled** the matter.
(Look it up in the NIV, and you'll know what I mean!
Hallelujah!) Mediate on this verse and write your thoughts.

Day #20
Today, God says I am Resurrected.

Jesus said to her, "I am the resurrection and the life.
The one who believes in me will live, even though they die;
and whoever lives by believing in me will never die.
Do you believe this?"
-John 11:25-26 NIV

My God is the God who calls dry bones to, "Come alive."
My God is the One who sees dead things as LIVING
possibilities—He alone makes the impossible, *possible* again!
With one word, the thing we thought was lost for good
can be restored to us, better than when we began.

His heart, His character is to **resurrect**—to make things new again.
To set things right.

Lord, thank You for starting with ME!
EVERLASTING LIFE!
No more death!
Thank You for rebuilding, for resetting, for making beautiful again
Thank You for the resurrecting work You are doing in my life today
I thank You, **in faith.**

Today, God says _____ is Resurrected.

Resurrected Journal Prompt:
Think of a specific situation needing God's help.
What do you want God to rebuild, reset,
and make beautiful once more? Write down these things.
Though God already knows them full well, pour out
your heart before Him in FAITH, certain of the
resurrection power He alone possesses.

Day #21
Today, God Says I am Heard.

Because he bends down to listen,
I will pray as long as I have breath!
-Psalm 116:2 NLT

Before the exodus took place—before Moses
led God's people out of the land of Egypt,
there is another verse that rings loudly in my heart.

. . . Their cry for rescue from slavery came up to God.
And God heard their groaning, and God remembered
his covenant with Abraham, with Isaac, and with Jacob.
God saw the people of Israel—and God knew.
-Exodus 2:23-25 ESV

My God HEARS. My God HEARS Me.

Lord, I thank You that You hear my cry. You hear every word I speak to You. You catch every tear that falls from my face and place each of them in a bottle, waiting for the DAY of redemption; the day of no more pain—no more tears. Thank You that You bend down to listen to Your kids. Thank You, that I can TRUST that You hear me every time—You are closer than a whisper away from me. Your heart is to show up for me.
Thank You for this, in Jesus Name. Amen.

Today, God Says _____ is Heard.

Heard Journal Prompt:
Read Psalm 18:6 in the New Living Translation.
1. Can you think of a time of distress when you called out to God in that moment?
2. Do you find yourself in a current circumstance of distress? Write about it with confidence that YOUR GOD hears you, every moment.

Week 3 Reflection

> **AFFIRMATIONS THIS WEEK:**
> STRENGTHENED, SAFE, CALMED,
> FORGIVEN, CLEAN, RESURRECTED, HEARD

1. Which affirmation spoke the most to you this week? Why?

___

2. Which affirmation this week could you grow in?

___

3. Are there any lies you've been believing that may have popped up this week while reading?
   - List them.
   - Talk to God about them.
   - Replace them with God's truth.
   - Thank God in advance for HELPING you live your life through a new lens of truth.

Day #22

TODAY, GOD SAYS I AM <u>HOPE-FULL</u>.

> Your road led through the sea,
> your pathway through the mighty waters—
> a pathway no one knew was there!
> -Psalm 77:19 NLT

A pathway no one knew was there!
THAT was the road God chose!

This verse—this promise—this TRUTH,
let it begin to permeate and mark my heart, God.

Let this verse become an ANCHOR of **hope** in my life. My God number #1—SEES roads, and ways out & *through,* which <u>no one else</u> has eyes to see! He Alone sees *options, solutions, provisions,* and *leads* well along the *right* paths for those who love Him and are seeking Him.

If I love Him, and am seeking Him, these roads that are *invisible* to the human imagination *will* become the roads God *lovingly* sets me on.

I am *hopeful* in Him. I am *hopeful* as I wait. *FULL of Hope.*

TODAY, GOD SAYS _____ IS HOPE-FULL.

HOPE-FULL JOURNAL PROMPT:
Read the whole chapter of Exodus 14.
It is the context of our theme verse for today.
Ask yourself and write down your answers:
1. What are the *impossible* roads I am asking God for?
Believing God for?
2. What are the difficult things I am *contending* for in my life?
Find your *courage* to keep believing.
You serve a creative, on-time, faithful God.

Day #23

TODAY, GOD SAYS I AM <u>FOUND</u>.

["]For the eyes of the LORD run to and fro throughout the whole earth, to show Himself strong on behalf of *those* whose heart *is* loyal to Him. . . ."
-2 Chronicles 16:9 NKJV

. . . to give strong support to those whose heart is blameless toward him. . . .
-2 Chronicles 16:9 ESV

God's promises are POWERFUL.

His Word **breaks through** the *lies* that knowingly or unknowingly we pick up along the way on our journey of life.

In times when I feel lost—lost in this world, or lost to myself, God says I am **always** FOUND.

He knows exactly where I am, exactly what I'm thinking, exactly how I'm struggling, and exactly what I'm contending with. He's never lost sight of me once. Not one time.

He is constantly *looking to and fro, throughout the whole earth,* looking for me, *to give strong support* because I've given Him my heart, making *my heart blameless toward Him.*

Help me find myself in Your Word, God.
Help me continue to believe every story in there is my story.

TODAY, GOD SAYS _____ IS FOUND.

<u>FOUND</u> JOURNAL PROMPT:
What other stories in the Bible come to mind, involving something that was once lost, but then was found again? Write down which stories / passages come to mind.
If you need a hint, here are some of my favorites:
Luke 15, Luke 8:43-48, Luke 18:35-42.

Day #24
TODAY, GOD SAYS I AM <u>HEALED.</u>

But he was pierced for our transgressions,
he was crushed for our iniquities; the punishment that
brought us peace was on him, and by his wounds we are healed.
-Isaiah 53:5 NIV

My God is the One who heals broken things.
Jesus, Himself was broken, so that He could FULLY understand my brokenness, and *take my brokenness from me*; removing what is way too heavy for me to carry.

He stands with me in the face of the fire.
He sits there with me in the cold.
He resets broken bones, wrapping me in His love, *as I wait.*

The punishment that brought us peace—broke Him.

AND by *these* wounds—His wounds, I am HEALED.

H A L L E L U J A H

TODAY, GOD SAYS _____ IS HEALED.

HEALED JOURNAL PROMPT:
From one friend to another, ask yourself, as I am:
1. Are there any broken things I need to give God today?
2. Are there any scattered pieces of my heart, my hopes, my dreams, my expectations, disappointments—*memories* I need to put into His hands and leave there, in trust today?

_____
_____
_____
_____
_____

Day #25
TODAY, GOD SAYS I AM **HEMMED IN**.

You hem me in, behind and before, and lay your hand upon me
Such knowledge is too wonderful for me; it is high;
I cannot attain it.
-Psalm 139:5-6 ESV

Picture a newborn swaddled in the warmest,
softest, fluffiest blanket. Now tell yourself,
"That's me. That's what my God promises to be for me."

"Hemmed in" in Biblical context meant:
"to be surrounded or besieged by God"
—that "He has us totally surrounded."

_{Killeen, Robin. "Hemmed in by God." Gulf Coast Woman Magazine, 2 Dec. 2020, www.gcwmultimedia.com/hemmed-in/?fbclid=IwZXh0bgNhZW0CMTAAAR731MJfPAVCRyWI_IkJ0UzuRI7-uw_3wxm_m8vuUakUzL3ixe8oaWISbTGsY aemPATzECsrk-yr4P1kb_i5Tg#:~:text=Psalms%20139%3A5%20says%3B%20%E2%80%9C,and%20directed%20by%20his%20han}

I am TOTALLY surrounded by my God.
If I am *entirely* surrounded by my God,
then I am *entirely* surrounded by His love, His mercy,
His strength, His peace, His goodness, His protection,
His provision, His presence, and more!
His attributes and characteristics go on forever.
Though I may not understand the path sometimes,
nor the process and *all* it entails, I can put a stake in the
ground knowing in my heart that I am hemmed in by my
Heavenly Father, the One who goes *before* me
—HE is the One who *goes with me.*

TODAY, GOD SAYS _____ IS HEMMED IN.

HEMMED IN JOURNAL PROMPT:
Where do you see evidence of God **surrounding** you this week?
Write these ways down. How can you see Him?

_____
_____
_____

Day #26
Today, God Says I am **Prayed For.**

Therefore he is able, once and forever,
to save those who come to God through him.
He lives forever to intercede with God on their behalf.
-Hebrews 7:25 NLT

"He lives forever to intercede with God on their behalf."
—Jesus' life is intercession forever—for me.
Read that about ten times.

... Christ Jesus is the one who died—more than that,
who was raised—who is at the right hand of God,
who indeed is interceding for us.
-Romans 8:34 ESV

Jesus lives on forevermore and I am promised that
He is at the right hand of the Father **praying** for me.

This encourages me. This strengthens me.
This uplifts my heart on hurting days.
No matter what I face on this side of eternity, I can find and build
my faith believing I am being prayed for every moment of
every day. I am upheld in prayer each day by Jesus Himself.
Every minute is accounted for.

And not a fleeting, half-dismissive prayer either.
He intercedes for me. He takes action to intervene on my behalf.

Today, God Says _____ is Prayed For.

Prayed For Journal Prompt:
Spend Time in John 17 today, the chapter where Jesus prayed for YOU. As you read Jesus' Words to His Father, be encouraged. Be comforted that your words may be simple and intimate to your Heavenly Father just as Jesus modeled. Express your gratitude in a written prayer below.

Day #27
Today, God Says I am **Anchored**.

We have this hope as an anchor for the soul, firm and secure.
It enters the inner sanctuary behind the curtain,
-Hebrews 6:19 NIV

This hope, this **anchor** for my soul, firm and secure, trustworthy, and steadfast is JESUS.

HE is the One who gives us access—HE is the One who gives me access into "the inner sanctuary behind the curtain".

On any stormy sea that I am caught upon,
I am **anchored** <u>in</u>, <u>by</u>, and <u>through</u> **Jesus**.

I can speak this, till I believe it. My God encourages me to mediate on His Words, over and over again, till they become *mine*, and make their way down *from my mind to my heart*.

It's as sure as the sun will rise.

I am *safely* anchored in, by, and through the person Jesus Christ. And **<u>nothing</u>**, and <u>no one</u> can take me from Him.

Today, God says _____ is Anchored.

Anchored Journal Prompt:

Ask yourself: Are there any lesser anchors I've picked up along the weary way? Are there any faulty anchors I've clung to, instead of my only true hope?

Write out a prayer of repentance if God shows you any anchors He wants to <u>erase</u> and <u>replace</u> with His SURE foundation and refuge for you.
He wants to give you REST, **real** rest.

_____
_____
_____
_____

Day #28
TODAY, GOD SAYS I AM FRUITFUL.

You did not choose me, but I chose you and appointed you
so that you might go and bear fruit—fruit that will last—and so
that whatever you ask in my name the Father will give you.
-John 15:16 NIV

Abide in Me, and I in you.
As the branch cannot bear fruit of itself,
unless it abides in the vine,
neither can you, unless you abide in Me.
-John 15:4 NKJV

My God calls me **fruitful.**

In His grace and His mercy, God called me, chose me
alongside His other beloved children, and appointed me,
so that I might go and bear lasting fruit of His fullness!
And then, praise God, He shows me the way to make this possible.

The *way* is a **Person**—the *way* is **The Way**.

As I abide in The Way—in Jesus—staying close to Him,
walking with Him, sitting, lingering in His Word & presence,
I will begin to bear lasting fruit of His Kingdom, fruit of His Spirit.

TODAY, GOD SAYS _____ IS FRUITFUL.

FRUITFUL JOURNAL PROMPT:
What is one small practical way you can abide a little more in
Jesus today? Write down what that looks like for you.

WEEK 4 REFLECTION

> **AFFIRMATIONS THIS WEEK:**
> HOPE-FULL, FOUND, HEALED,
> HEMMED IN, PRAYED FOR, ANCHORED, FRUITFUL

1. Which affirmation spoke the most to you this week? Why?
___
___
___
___
___
___
___

2. Which affirmation this week could you grow in?
___
___
___
___
___
___
___
___
___
___

3. Are there any lies you've been believing that may have popped up this week while reading?
   - List them.
   - Talk to God about them.
   - Replace them with God's truth.
   - Thank God in advance for HELPING you live your life through a new lens of truth.

Day #29

TODAY, GOD SAYS I AM <u>EQUIPPED</u>.

All Scripture is breathed out by God and profitable for teaching, for reproof, for correction, and for training in righteousness, that the man of God may be complete, equipped for every good work.
-2 Timothy 3:16-17 ESV

[S]o that the man of God may be adequate,
equipped for every good work.
-2 Timothy 3:17 NASB1995

In a world which constantly bombards us with *messages* that <u>stress</u>:
"I am not good enough", "I am not qualified enough",
"I don't have enough of ____", "I don't know the right people".
God's Word says, I have been "equipped for every good work".
Though the world's voices are loud and can feel overbearing,
I can remember WHO overshadows them all—whose
voice **remains** to carry the weight of stilling
the waves and wind, **settling the matter**.

God's Word is our weapon. The Bible is our instructions.
It is perfect and breathed by God, *penned* by His beloved
servants who gave their lives to following that oh so *holy call*.

In the same way, when I said *yes* to Christ and became His
"trainee in progress" as 2 Timothy says, God *has* equipped me,
and <u>is</u> **equipping** me, that I may become complete in
Him for every good plan He's marked for me.

Hallelujah—Amen—thank You Father for giving me all I need!

TODAY, GOD SAYS _____ IS EQUIPPED.

<u>EQUIPPED</u> JOURNAL PROMPT:
What lies have the world been telling you? What are the mixed messages you knowingly or unknowingly have let in from the enemy? Make some time to do the work with God on this. Write out the lies & then write out Truths from what God says about you in His Word contradicting those lies. Take ALL of this to God & see how He re-writes your stories.

LIES	TRUTH

Day #30
TODAY, GOD SAYS I AM <u>THOUGHT OF.</u>

For I know the thoughts that I think toward you, says the LORD thoughts of peace and not of evil, to give you a future and a hope
-Jeremiah 29:11 NKJV

"Thoughts of peace and not of evil."
May these words quiet my heart and calm my mind.
They are Truth. God's Word is EVERYTHING.

God has good plans and purposes for me
—plans and purposes to give a future and a hope.

How abundant are the good things that you have stored up for those who fear you, that you bestow in the sight of all, on those who take refuge in you.
-Psalm 31:19 NIV

When plans change suddenly to my eyes, and <u>my</u> understanding, Lord HELP me turn back to Your Word to *renew my strength, silence my accusers, lift my eyes,* and *heal my heart.*

HELP me remember: **You are never far from me**.
Psalm 139 assures me of this.

TODAY, GOD SAYS _____ IS THOUGHT OF.

FRUITFUL JOURNAL PROMPT:
Read Psalm 139 in its entirety. These are some of God's thoughts about YOU. Write a few things down:
1. Did any verse particularly stand out to you?
2. Were there any "thoughts" God has about you that are new to you?
3. What is one attribute / characteristic of God you see in this chapter?

Day #31

Today, God says I am <u>Commissioned</u>.

And Jesus came and spoke to them, saying,
"All authority has been given to Me in heaven and on earth.
Go therefore and make disciples of all the nations, baptizing
them in the name of the Father and of the Son and of the Holy
Spirit, teaching them to observe all things that I have commanded
you; and lo, I am with you always, *even* to the end of the age."
Amen.
-Matthew 28:18-20 NKJV

The last thing Jesus said,
is the last thing I will read, in this devotional.

My God has **commissioned me.**

I am included in the mission & purpose of Jesus:
being born in a manger,
living & restoring here on earth,
dying on the cross—being <u>our</u> Sacrifice,
raising to life again, and living on for all of *eternity.*
God saw it fit to invite *me* to *help further*
the beautiful work of *Jesus.*

Today, God says to Me:

_____,

Partner with Me—*go therefore and make disciples of all the nations.*
Baptize them (or bring them where they can be baptized)
in the name of the *Father, of the Son, and of the Holy Spirit.*
Teach them to observe all I have commanded you.
And never forget, *I am with you always,*
even to the end of the age. Amen.

You are commissioned. You have purpose. You are loved.
Therefore, GO.

Commissioned Journal Prompt:
Pray this simple prayer and write down what God says to you.
Write down the thoughts that come to mind.
**Lord, Today, You've commissioned me. What is the first step
You would have me take for Your Kingdom and Your Glory?**

Week 5 Final Reflection

> ## Affirmations This Week:
> ### Equipped, Thought Of, Commissioned

1. Which affirmation spoke the most to you this week? Why?

_____
_____
_____
_____
_____
_____
_____

2. Which affirmation this week could you grow in?

_____
_____
_____
_____
_____
_____
_____
_____
_____

3. Are there any lies you've been believing that may have popped up this week while reading?
   - List them.
   - Talk to God about them.
   - Replace them with God's truth.
   - Thank God in advance for HELPING you live your life through a new lens of truth.

4. We've now concluded our journey together. Congratulations & THANK YOU. Write down one lesson—one take away you've learned along the way about who God says you are.

_____
_____
_____
_____
_____
_____
_____
_____
_____
_____
_____

5. Write down one piece of encouragement you've received from this devotional you can pass along to someone in your life.

_____
_____
_____
_____
_____
_____
_____
_____
_____
_____
_____
_____
_____
_____

Invitation

No matter how you came across this devotional,
here you are—you've reached the end. Congratulations!

I couldn't end our time together without including a Salvation
Prayer, asking Jesus into your heart and into your life.
1 John 4:9-10 NLT beautifully puts it like this:

God showed how much he loved us by sending
his one and only Son into the world so that we
might have eternal life through him.
This is real love—not that we loved God,
but that he loved us and sent his Son
as a sacrifice to take away our sins.

Maybe you've read through this devotional and some,
or *much* of this information you are hearing for the first time.
You may not understand it all,
but you feel in your heart a *response* . . .

Q: What is the *next step*?

A: The Prayer of Salvation.

PRAYER OF SALVATION

Pray with me:

Dear God,

Though I don't really know You yet, I have come to know on this journey who You say that I am. I am loved. I am seen. I am chosen by You.

I thank You for loving me even before I knew to love You back. Thank You for seeing me even when I didn't know to look for You. Thank You for choosing me before I said *yes* to You.

Jesus, thank You for giving up Your life as a sacrifice on the cross for me. Forgive me for my sins—for the wrongs that I've done. I am sorry and I ask for Your forgiveness. I ask You to forgive me and wash me clean today.

Please come into my heart. Be my Savior and Lord of my life. Be my Shepherd. Help me walk with You. Show me the way forward.

In Jesus' name,
Amen.

If you prayed this prayer for the first time, or as a rededication moment with the Lord, scan the QR code for a special resource from me.

ACKNOWLEDGEMENTS

To my wonderful family—Joe, Tracey, and Gabriella,
who inspire me to keep on going, love me, stand with me, and are
my BIGGEST cheerleaders in everything God sets before me.
I thank God for you!

There were a few key individuals
with me on the journey of creating this devotional:
To my Mom, thank you for having that conversation with me—
one conversation, inspired by the Lord,
to give me the idea and push to start writing.
Thank you!

To Nancy, for always inviting me to Dream as we'd meet
for coffee. For brainstorming with me and believing
that I could do big things.
Thank you!

To a very special individual who caught the vision of this
devotional from the beginning and said, "Let's get this thing
published!" I cannot thank you enough for your kindness
and JOY in helping bring this dream to fruition.
Thank you!

To those who have given, sown seeds, and supported
what the Lord has done in my life through this project—
my first published book!
Thank you!

To Diana Robinson and Transformed Publishing
for welcoming me in; for your giftings and guidance.
Thank you!

With SO much gratitude:
To Jesus, who filled my fingers with His Words to write,
who fills the hungry with good things (*see* Luke 1:53),
and who brings peace & JOY to my heart.
I thank You!

ABOUT THE AUTHOR

Briley Jo Cruz, devoted to her love for Jesus and "seeking first" His kingdom (*see* Matt. 6:33), loves to worship, create, explore new places, and laugh with those she loves. She is passionate about God's Word and giving out to others what God has given her.

Raised in a family who loves Jesus, from a very young age, God began to carve out her heart for people, children, and nations. The vision is multiple: *mission to mission, assignment to assignment,* as the Lord leads.

Her writing journey began after a firsthand experience with bullying in high school, where God began to sing songs of deliverance over her, songs of healing and hope.
Her music ministry continued, giving way to writing devotional style blog posts encouraging readers all over the world. And now, the next chapter: *Today God Says I Am.* This gift of understanding identity in a new light through her own walk with Christ INSPIRES her to shout it from the rooftops and let the love of the Lord be known.

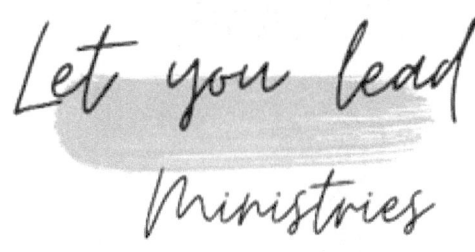

B R I L E Y   J O   C R U Z

Briley Jo Cruz | Let You Lead Ministries
"Out of the overflow of what God gives, we give to others. Helping people. Praising JESUS all the way."

Resources & Ways To Connect:

Website:
letyouleadme.wordpress.com

Blog Cites:
letyoulead.wordpress.com
mtntopthisway.wordpress.com

Email:
letyouleadbjc@gmail.com

YouTube:
@letyouleadbjc

Facebook:
@brileyjocruz

Instagram:
@letyouleadbjc

www.ingramcontent.com/pod-product-compliance
Lightning Source LLC
Chambersburg PA
CBHW020249010526
44107CB00002B/168